LOSING
MOGADISHU

LOSING
MOGADISHU

Mark E. Harden

authorHOUSE®

AuthorHouse™
1663 Liberty Drive
Bloomington, IN 47403
www.authorhouse.com
Phone: 1 (800) 839-8640

Published by AuthorHouse 04/23/2015

ISBN: 978-1-5049-0844-3 (sc)
ISBN: 978-1-5049-0843-6 (e)

Library of Congress Control Number: 2015906320

Print information available on the last page.

Dedication Page

To all who heard the pipes and answered the call,
and especially to the veterans of
Somalia-

You are not forgotten.

No Reason

This very night
an owl
spoke
three times

then was gone-

in the autumn twilight
beneath the arbor's browning
trumpet vine
and falling blossoms

we listened for it in the stillness,

you wondered aloud of the reason for its flight

as I wonder alone of mine

before the war,
when our shared silence
was woven with unspoken knowing
I could have told you…

You need to remember that-

be careful not to drift
too far from the edge of this moment

and ask why I've not come home

…hard to explain how I see it all sometimes…it's like I'm looking at an image of someone looking in a mirror…I don't know if the reflection goes on forever or just as far as my mind allows it to…perhaps I just don't want to look too deeply…maybe I'm afraid to admit that the image doesn't really go anywhere…

…can't imagine it might get any more quiet here…I have a fairly large house- single story, wide open floor plan…lots of subdued lighting to help me get around it in the evening…don't much care for illumination, at least literally…odd though that I don't do well in the dark anymore either…half of me wants to see…the other half doesn't even want to look, resigned with lying to myself that I've seen it all before…

…weather channel's on mute but the red and yellow radar colors are shrill enough…more storms up north in Oklahoma…another bright band of misery is rolling into St. Louis- all I know of that city is the airport- caught many a MAC flight out of it….said goodbye to someone there once that I never saw again…I still think about that…

…it's a warm evening…think I'll move on out to the arbor…a few clouds are slowly passing over, taunting a silver moon …just enough light to see the shadows- dark enough to hide from everything else…

Don't Look

loaded to capacity with fatigued
hollow eyed troopers

the chartered aircraft
went wheels up from the Mog
Christmas Eve

soaring swiftly away from a debris field
littered with abandoned aircraft

tangled, rusting wire
rotting sandbags

empty buildings
echoes of slogans

restore hope

leave no one behind-

like a photo
of a mirror in a mirror

I sometimes find myself
staring at the illusion of it all

the false sense of depth,

endless reflection

...cold out today...seems that the new year always begins like this... rain, sleet...did manage to make a couple of resolutions...one of 'em was to not worry about breaking any...

...Christmas came a little late for some of my veterans...strike that-should read OUR veterans...advance GI Bill pay checks finally arrived Monday...

...one fellow stopped by to get his...was carrying a teacup dog in the pocket of his faded, tattered pea coat...talked to the tiny companion the whole time we were processing the paperwork...as I handed him the check, he told it that they were going to get some good, canned dog food and celebrate...after they left one of my assistants remarked to me that his cologne was overpowering......

...and in that instant I fell away from Austin and found myself back in Mogadishu, standing close to another person that reeked horribly of perfume in a feeble attempt to mask another smell...someone desperately looking for a way out of her situation...I couldn't help her...or her husband...or their young daughter...

...been home two hours now, listenin' to some Joan Osborne blues and nearing the bottom of a bottle of Prosecco...

...when I close my eyes, I can still see them...

Trade

all dolled up for the pitch
in a wilted red dress

reeking of perfume

the razor-thin Somali who dragged away our dung

offered to trade,

from an open palm
skeletal fingers
unwrapped
a silk scarf

revealing
a string of luminescent pearls-

I saw her later
in the shadow of the tower

fists clenched

grinding her bones

…that's the thing about ghosts- you never know when they're going to show up, and they never tell you how long they intend to stay… sometimes they play tag-team with one another…just as soon as you begin to wear one out, another reaches into the ring to take his place…

…someone asked me once which memory of Mogadishu, which single event in that godforsaken city defined my experience…a couple of recollections came to mind- one was a mortar attack- another spoke to the airfield on Oct. 3rd…there are more, but those seemed the most immediate…

…as always, though, I've let the question simmer- found myself rifling through my shoebox of mental snapshots, looking for the one that really captures the essence of how it was…in my searching there are two images that keep floating to the top of the pile…I've seen them both more than once in my dreams-

…one is that of a small child rolling a hubcap in the dirt road with a stick as our convoy headed toward Sword Base the first day…I was soon to learn how lethal that adolescent could be…

…and then there's that last day…riding in the cargo bed of a five ton truck, looking back with emotional detachment at what might have been the same kid standing alone on that same dirt road, waving goodbye…

…how do you explain to someone back in the world that you've lost faith in damn near everything, even children…

…there's no sense trying…

…severe storms in central Texas this evening…I've been expecting those…

Counting Coup in Mogadishu

it is a graceful combination of speed and strength

nearly sublime

as the thin, dark skinned boy
raises his rifle from within the swelling throng

lift and aim, smoothly

stock to cheek, grip relaxed

breathe in, half out

squeeze, don't pull

click-

rehearsed again and again
while chewing khat,

I react poorly

heavy and slow

too old, too dull to respect his skill
or my depreciation

but I just see
as he melts easily back into the closing crowd

a flash of smile

... my mother moved on yesterday- got the call from my sister around 10 PM…how plain those words look on this page…"moved on"…oh, that it could it be so simple- then again, perhaps it is…perhaps she really has finally boarded her train to some destination better than where she'd been most of her earthly life- one can only hope…

…stopped by the VFW after work…had a couple of colds ones with an acquaintance…we toasted the old gal once or twice and that was that…I'll be heading back to Indiana next week to stamp "Closed" on this part in my life…if only some of my other episodes might conclude this cleanly…

……this is what I wish for my mother…

…I hope her train has returned her to that early summer of 1950, back to a time when she was sitting in the Fine Arts building at Indiana State University sketching a pencil portrait of her soon-to-be husband, my old man…

…before the Korean War, before that wondrous pool of innocence began to drain away and the concrete foundation of despair replaced it…I hope she's there now, enjoying a time when life was so full with future, so huge with expectation…when it was fun to dream about tomorrow, when another sunrise meant promise, not redundancy…I hope she's onboard that train…if anyone deserves to be, it's her…

…Doris Day had it right, although I'm not too much into taking a sentimental journey right now-

> "seven, that's the time we leave, at seven,
> I'll be waiting up for heaven, counting every mile,
> of railroad track, that takes me back…"

I hope she's done counting the miles…

Saturday Nights

it was an old house, circa 1930's,

well built, weathered
white with rusting wrought iron porch railings
facing St. Ann's-

she would often return first

slurring and mumbling as
she fumbled for her keys,
finally lurching into the foyer -

then him, usually minutes later

locked out and shouting
as he stumbled to the back yard
to enter through the kitchen-

the rooms were spacious, with heavy oak doors
set in splintered jambs

they would slam shut again and again
with drunken energy

explosions that seemed to suck
the air out of my lungs

while I hid under the sheet
and lied to God

…I don't know why things come upon me…why I would remember a moment in time, a fragment of a conversation with someone decades ago…maybe it's all this talk of war in the Korean peninsula…...I grow so weary of drums, but at the same time I find myself listening to the beat and moving toward the sound…can't explain it…I can only write about it and then wonder why I felt a need to search for the words…

…turned the news off and decided to move to the backyard…while tippin' a cold one and enjoying the twilight I began thinking about my uncle Dick…I used to cut his grass when I was a kid…one time after I finished he took me to his sanctuary- a small attic alcove…scarcely enough room for one person, let alone two…it was there where he spent time making fly fishing lures-he showed me his miniature vice, the feathers he used, the different colors of thread, the tiny fishing hooks…it must have been a difficult task for him as his left hand was severely damaged by a German machine gun during the Battle of the Bulge- eavesdropping on small talk at family gatherings I'd heard that the hand was the least worrisome of his injuries…

…before we left, I asked him how long it took him to make a fly…he said to me that he really wasn't sure…he only knew when one was finished…

…I found the whole thing a little boring…why would someone want to spend hours in a tiny space, struggling to wrap string around a metal fishing hook…?

…I once watched my old man working on an ancient spinning reel in our basement on Locust…worried over it for hours…I used to wonder why he gave such attention to an obsolete reel… something broken that wasn't supposed to be worth the effort to repair and make useful again…

…I get it now…

…I wish I could talk to him about that…

Lesson

a poor imitation of its namesake,
its fiberglass blades fractured beyond repair,

the broken Black Hawk plummets-

Icarus found

that folly trumps technology...
be them titanium or wax,

wings will fail-

no man may glide free
on warm sea winds

…well, as spring is wont to do, she's decided change…the sun's gone, and along with it the warmth I was partially basking in beneath the pergola…I've moved back to the kitchen- funny how the departure of some thin shadows can shift a mood so subtly…

…been revising a little poetry…working with the space between the lines…they call it white space…that distance between one thought and the next…an empty line that reveals so much but can be so misunderstood…

…transitioning is easy… to transition is hard…some folks are ever crossing a river, at least figuratively…I have sympathy for those struggling in the current but I have compassion too for the ones that never leave the bank…it's a hard thing, it is, going from one side to the next…I know a little of that…

….one of my students emailed me this morning before the exam… wrote that he couldn't find his review and he usually studied the morning of the test-asked me to call him…if it was anyone other than this individual I'd probably chalk it up to a high speed who'd spent too much time in the taverns last night on Austin's 6th street…

…but this fellow's a veteran…U.S. Army 11 Bravo- straight leg as they come…two tours in Iraq and one in Afghanistan…I have his DD214- I know what he's done for my country- scratch that- OUR country…he suffers from a host of things- TBI, PTS…struggles in class to communicate…

…I'd guess there's a whole world of white space between the person he was and the person he is now…he might be in the river forever…

…I called him…told him no problem…I'd send him another review Monday- he could take the test before class next Saturday…

…there's a bottle of Pietra Santa next to me on the table…it's short by one glass…I'm going to improve the odds of it being empty by late evening…

# Bird On a Wire

after the mortar attack
I decided to check on Private Shownower

a skinny, beak nosed kid with owlish eyes
perched in a plywood cage lined with sandbags
atop two stacked cargo containers

taking a last deep drag
on a bummed Salem

I hauled myself a rung at a time
up the guard post ladder
to share his bird's eye view
of the ruin and ruble across the road,

as we stared into the twilight
a truck overflowing with Somali's
rattled past our position

one of the riders
let loose with his rifle

the rounds ricocheting
off the church tower bell behind us

Shownower, stammering,
asked if I was scared…

I wondered if he was a smoker yet-

…while we were enjoying our Memorial Day, a soldier from Burnett, Texas died in Afghanistan…

…I did a search to see what else I could find out about him…not too many details in the news…he played trombone in his high school band…liked to listen to Christian music…had a brother, sister…served with the 101st ABN out of FTCKY, my old stompin' grounds…

…oh, and he was 19 years old…

…I think about all the things I've done since I was 19…all the wins, the losses…the places I've been, things I've seen, people I've loved and the ones I did not- I might spend too much time on that one-

…I think of all the lives I've touched, either lightly or with a sledge…I can smile at the opportunities I've had and smile more broadly at the ones I had the good fortune to miss…

…woke up this morning and it was still with me- I couldn't tell you why…over coffee I found myself remembering a PFC named Jonas, a sandy-haired kid who was my driver and the youngest of the troopers I led and did my best to safeguard in Mogadishu- Jonas was full of that fearlessness, that invincibility all young war fighters simply assume they possess…call it grace if you like or call it luck, but we all came home…

…ah, but that last line has a qualifier…I can only speak for myself but sometimes it feels like I've left something behind- something that didn't make it on the plane with me when I boarded…sometimes I've found myself wishing I could go back and get it…

…I wish too I'd known this young man…

...followed my usual Saturday routine to try and shake all of this off- mowed the backyard and mulched everything but the grass itself... hit the treadmill in the gym for a change- five miles as hard as I can run 'em on a machine with artificial hills throughout...stopped by the store for six pack of Shiner's...

...but none of that has made a whole lot of difference...all of this is still with me...guess I'll just twist open another bottle and move on out to the arbor...shadows are starting to fall...

...won't be long before the locusts begin to sing...

Flight Plan

muezzin's evening call to worship
echoes across the base,

haunting notes that
drift like incense…

I find the distant
staccato chant

of
automatic weapon fire
a more soothing sermon
as it mixes with the faint aroma of cordite,

a single parachute flare
floats weakly above the far end of the runway

the illumination nearly lost to a full moon

no one speaks of
tomorrows flight

or

the flag-covered
containers aligned dress right dress in the hanger

those belong to the loadmaster

…got a good start on the weekend…up early to cut the grass, worked in a 5.5 mile run, cooled off in the back yard with a glass of ice tea and even managed to get in a little writing…soon I'll be off to the post for a couple of cold ones…with any luck, I'll get there before Charlie does so I can buy the first round…

…Charlie is a Navy Vietnam vet who served on the USS Goldsborough, DDG-20, from 1967 to 1970…easy enough to read about his boat if you search the net a little…

…what you can't read about is how Charlie's tour affected him…none of us really know- he doesn't talk much about it- but every once in a while he lets us on board his old ship, shows us around and reminisces about the good times- when his voice starts to break, someone raises a glass to toast the Irish and we all come back…

…we were swapping stories about music one afternoon and I mentioned a couple of tunes I knew from the late 1960's…Charlie said that the only one he really remembered was the Letter, by the Box Tops…I asked him how it was that he was so familiar with that particular song…his reply- whenever the Goldsborough had a fire mission it was piped through the intercom system…couldn't remember them ever firing without it…he said that hardly a day went by without him thinking about that song…

…I heard his throat catch as he started to sing…

"Gimme a ticket for an aeroplane,
Ain't got time to take a fast train.
Lonely days are gone, I'm a-goin' home,
'Cause my baby just a-wrote me a letter."

…someone called out a toast to the Irish-

No Exit

I think about Charlie now and then

ever moored to a bar stool in the VFW
listing to starboard and chasing shots

sweating in the belly of the USS Goldberg
while it lobs seventy pounders into North Vietnam

he slurred to me once that during every fire mission
they played the old Box Tops tune the Letter
on the ship intercom

said that not a day goes by when he doesn't hear that song,

I still remember my buddy Roy sitting on the ground
outside Headquarters on Hunter Base

field striping his M16
running a toothbrush around the inside of the bolt carrier

blowing a little Mogadishu sand off the stock,

he looked up at me and mumbled
"man, one dude had a chunk of RPG in him

he's is in a graves registration reefer van
waitin' on EOD"

so many
small fragments
of emotional shrapnel

struggling to break the surface
when some random thought sets them in motion

there's almost never an exit wound

…read an article recently about Omaha Beach…a Texas geologist visited it decades ago- brought back some sand…discovered that mixed in with the small grains of rock were tiny particles of metal shrapnel- fragmented, rusting, man-made contributions to the ecological environment…

…the scientist made the observation that in a century or so it would all be gone- the metal, the rust, the jagged pieces of history that speak only of the dead…nothing left save a few silent memorials to attest to that horrific day, June 6th, 1944-

…perhaps he's right…it could be that he is optimistic about the hundred years…

…sometimes I wonder if the souls of the men that fought and died on that relatively small stretch of coastline are still traveling, still trying to distance themselves from such a tragic moment in time and space… if the cries of anguish and despair, of fear and anger are still moving away from us, growing fainter as their ripples extend…

…It's been said that some things are infinite…I hope that love is…

…I surely pray that suffering is not…

 Missing

they are still there-

so many

lost in seasons of snow and ice
monsoon and sun

falling inexorably
to fragments of tooth and bone

their names buried deep in the marrow-

once

on a frigid winter evening
sipping Soju to stay warm
near the south bank of the frozen Imjin

I heard them
whispering an ancient Sirens song
high into the wind

such cold, sorrowful music,

pleading with me to stay

warning me not to sleep

…I wonder sometimes about walls…Frost asked us if they really made for good neighbors, stating that "something there is that doesn't love a wall"- I might claim little use for them yet at the same time it seems that I've always had a need to keep them around me…

…I knew a woman once…ours was a short run…we built walls for ourselves, thinking that they were necessary…yet we never disclosed to one another our reasons- by the end of it the walls didn't exist for us- they became us…

…driving to work this morning, hugging the barrier in the left lane as I alternately raced and crawled in the traffic, I thought about walls- I've stood watch on a few, patrolled a couple, guarded one or two… I never minded the duty- it was simple, clean, honest, honorable work- I understood it…all of us understood it…

… I still stand watch over walls I suppose, but there seems no particular purpose to it anymore…

…I've written a poem or two…when I look back over one I always see the wall I built while writing it-

…the poem moves on, as is its nature…

…the wall remains…

 **Gun Line**

she whispered to me once
that colors could sing

like wind at dusk
she felt the shadowed notes
brush against her bare skin

soft maroon and mauve scarves
that echoed far into the fading summer sky,

from a thousand miles away
through a thin crackling connection

a scrabbled fragment of voice
rough and dry as desert sand
asked when I was coming home,

soon, I lied

as I waited on the line
for another starless night
thick with cloud
to wash me
in fierce waves
of percussion and flash

violent ripples of sound
circling upward into the dark

…Sunday is Father's Day…it isn't a holiday I particularly like…hard to explain why…

…I keep an old Polaroid that most represents my relationship with my old man- a snapshot I took of him standing on the bank of a pond as I floated away in a small rowboat…

…Pop left me with many things…he taught me to love singing for the sake of singing…the way to fold a flag…how to sit on a porch and watch a storm sweep in and bend the trees…he showed me how to anchor a boat and cast a line…he taught me how to visit a saloon and become a part of it…

…although he never knew it, he taught me that everything is finite- many things come and end too quickly- from him I learned that I should not aspire to be like him but to be like myself- that I should not treat women as he treated my mother…

…years later I realized that Pop had true love for most things but he never found a way to love himself…something that maybe all of us might work on…

…so, at the end of it, I'm guess I'm still alone in that boat in the photo, as perhaps are we all…who knows, maybe your father's still on a shore somewhere and you, like me, are still pretending to row away, pretending to be in control of your direction as you drift…

…good luck with your Father's Day…

Because, Just Because

snapping his fingers, and singing, *"just 'cause you think you're so pretty"*,
he points to his empty glass…
Shirley wobbles over to the sticky countertop
to mix him another-
a double shot of Seagrams splashed with coke…

"I ever tell you about the time", he'd say to me,
leaning back in his captains chair,
pounding a new pack of smokes on his palm,

"I beat Pete the Greek, six-love, six-love,
on the clay at Collett Park,
not even a month back from action…

aced him match point,
then pitched him the other ball-
sonofabitch never could play…"
he'd exhale, disappearing behind the
blue Lucky Strike smoke…

I bought him a racquet,
six ply, medium grip, with press,
from Poff's Sporting Goods up on Twelve Points,
gave it to him, along with a can of Wilsons,
early one afternoon
before they started on a new bottle of VO-

we rattled down Layfette in our rusted Galaxy
to a gymnasium wall
where I dualed every day
against Stan Smith…
we pulled up, and Pop steered Shirley toward the bait shop across
the street

to get more ice and coke…

he stood ten, maybe twelve feet from the brick,
balancing the ball on the racquet head,
then he flipped it toward the wall
and watched it bounce back…
he met it waist high
and smacked it hard with an open stroke…

bending low and swinging the racquet up,
he began to build some rhythm,
shifting gracefully from forehand to backhand,
the ball hitting just above a frayed piece of tape…

I stood wide eyed as the yellow blur
snapped back to the racquet's sweet spot,
again and again,
tethered by an invisible rubber band…

for a moment there was only the sharp crack
of the ball whistling into the wall,
and Pop's deck shoes scraping on the hot concrete…
if I closed my eyes, it might be Forest Hills,
the old man and Stan Smith on center court…

then he stopped…
I hadn't even noticed the spent cigarette,
until he flicked it away,
he snapped his fingers, and Shirley
stumbled out of her lawn chair, his drink in hand,

"we're going to Collet Park", he said,
"lets see what you got…"
and he started singing again…

"I'm tellin' you, baby, I'm through with you…because, just because"

...it's very still outside...perhaps a lull before a storm- they're forecast this evening...I'm sitting in the backyard, practicing long, slow pulls from my sweating bottled beer and watching my tiny hummingbirds dart from flower to flower in search of one more drink before nightfall- fortunately, I'm not bound by those rules...trumpet vines are still in bloom, although I'm not sure how many more times my small friends can drink from those wells...

...I've come to the conclusion that my Bradford Pear trees were planted too close together, as they're touching branches now...in the grand scheme of things maybe it wasn't a mistake after all...some things need to touch one another...

...logged 25 running miles this week...my bones feel it- but the running keeps the ghosts behind me, at least most of the time...they don't train as hard as I, so it really irritates me when I find one in front of me after all the hard work I've put in...ah, but that's the way of it- you can't outrun your past, or anyone else's, for that matter...

...heard this morning that an El Paso soldier was killed in Afghanistan last week...left behind a wife, two kids...month out from redeploying... ending his fourth combat tour- one in Iraq and two previous trips in Afghanistan...

...lots of clouds in the sky...not quite dark yet...I still hear a few birds... there's a little locust music playing in the background...it strikes me that sitting out here on a humid Texas evening, enjoying a cold Shiner while I watch the shadows grow, I can almost convince myself that I don't really miss the days when I was so fortunate to share company with heroes like our forever young Texan...

…ah well, whoever you are, wherever you are, count your blessings… count 'em now…don't wait another moment…kiss your significant other, hold your child tight…call someone that you've been irritated at…take that rusty hatchet and drop it in a hole…

…let it go…let it all go……

Veterans Cemetery

I wait beneath a
half moon sky

with wind filled trees
whose rasping sighs

are wistful songs
of textured cord
no melancholy could afford...

but there's no one here
to cross with me

this meadow
dark with harmony

a pasture rich in broken bone
where widows speak
to silent stone

their shadows spill from end to end,

their whispers fill this grieving glen-

…dreamt the night before last that I was back in Korea, patrolling roads and bridges up along the DMZ…couldn't tell you why…I ended my third tour in '97…I had a pretty good time there, especially with the Artillery and with the CAV but I've no particular reason to look back…

…was checking the mail after work the next day- found an envelope from my sister, who's moving to Antigua…enclosed, some items from the past…a couple childhood photos of me…a few poems I composed when I was in grade school…

…and two Army photos of my old man taken in Korea…

…the first photo was probably circa late 40's…Pop's in a dress uniform, sitting with some young Korean children…he looks like a kid himself… probably 21, maybe 22 years old…got back to the states in '49 and started college that spring of 1950…wanted to be an English teacher…

…the second photo was dated on the back…May of 1951- he's in fatigues and combat boots…been in country again since October of 50' with a Heavy Mortar Company, 7th Infantry Regiment, 3rd Division…

…not many of his old friends knew he'd been gone……no one, except perhaps his young bride realized that a part of him didn't make it all the way back…

…holding the faded snapshot of my old man up close I could see it though, there in the eyes- I know the look…the kid was gone, lost somewhere on that frozen road from Chosin…

…maybe he was trying to tell me something the night before last, while I slept…or maybe I was trying to say something to him…who knows…

…ah, but it's hot here in Texas…Pop would have liked it…maybe I'll sit out under the arbor tonight while it's still 95 degrees…bring an extra beer with me just in case that ghost decides to pay me a visit…

 Korean War Memorial

visit
only when you are weary of winter
and hopeless with fatigue

and then too, only at dusk,
as shadows of the statues sink into the abyss,

to share the dark despair of those desperate souls
cast into such a cold Asian hell

on the road from Chosin…

where wind driven scythes
of sleet and snow and Communist Chinese

barreled screaming
down nameless numbered ridges
and barren hills,
slicing through the struggling squads of soldiers, Marines

all trapped

like the apparitions etched on this granite wall-

forever to wait
for the false warmth of a
bleak sunrise…

…a friend of mine, a Scot, aspiring novelist and poet wrote recently of the passing of the firefly season…

…I've always thought fireflies to be magical creatures, right up there with Unicorns…I had not realized how I'd so missed them…sitting under the arbor last night it occurred to me that perhaps I was to blame for their disappearance from my life…I too wrote a piece about them once during an especially challenging time…

…maybe it was they sensed that the dark place I was living in would not permit any light, especially theirs…that beautiful, erratic, fleetingly illuminative lover's call they were sending to one another…perhaps they interpreted my words to be more than metaphor- collectively fearful I'd truly do that which I wrote- end their communication… in any event they haven't returned…perhaps someday they will…or not…the loss is certainly mine…it's not my first…

…but it's Friday…the beginning of another brief respite…and it's a scorcher outside…July has apparently been the hottest month ever in Austin…when it drops to 80 degrees it'll feel cold…

…I'm thinkin' about hittin' the bricks for a long run…then I just may treat myself to a pint of Guinness…move to the backyard and sit out in the open, away from the arbor's trumpet vine canopy…watch for falling stars…

…if I'm lucky, maybe someone will let the fireflies know that I'm sorry…

…I'd tell 'em myself but I've just never been very good at that sort of thing…

Running Away

it's not as if I can't go back

if I want

all I really need is
a nervous half-moon night

some scattered clouds

Black Hawks fly low over the trees
I never see them in the dark

paths wind
beneath Shell Road bridge
to the San Gabriel

cars boom overhead

like artillery
far off in the distance
my heart pounds as I run

…by the end of a week like this one words just seem to lose their significance- I've heard so many of them, had so many conversations on the phone ……even email seems to bring its own amplification… just want to turn the volume down inside and outside my head…

…this I can tell you- there are an awful lot of veterans out there struggling right now…and not just OIF/OEF folks…older veterans, too… out of work, out of money, no home, no family…they all seem to share one thing, though- a growing sense of isolation and resignation…they feel abandoned…

…I've spoken to over a dozen in person the past three days…well, I've listened more than I've talked…each poor soul's story has been different, but all of them carry the same message- they need help… real help…

…one fellow, a 54 year old homeless Army vet, broke down in my office today- I watched him struggle with his emotions for a good three or four minutes until the damn burst and the tears streamed down his face…he'd been describing how things began to fall apart a few years ago, beginning with the slow death of his wife…he apologized, saying that he didn't know why he'd lost his composure- he'd been so good at keeping those memories locked away…

…I said no one could expect him to keep it all boarded up forever…I'd been there myself…sometimes even the smallest of things could still occasionally bring me to tears…he'd be ok…

…I almost told him the truth-

…I'm so weary of words…

Thief

I heard her calling again last night,
searching for me

that sightless, stumbling Barrabbas

parched voice whispering harsh, brittle words,
stirring memories soundless as Braille…

she carries her handicap too humbly, though,

I understand well her loss of vision

why she stays

how it is she still sleeps in this windblown, ageless bed…

and I have seen her more than once at sunset,
resting on her dry ocean floor

a rough, eroded stone
prisoner to her solitude…

but I know what will happen soon, so soon-

she will steal once more
when she finds me

kneeling by this shadowed crescent shore,

cruel and empty

while imaginary waves lap at her feet
and stain the pale, desert sand…

…I saw the movie Gran Torino yesterday…

…the main character stirred up the ghost of my old man, the real life Korean War veteran and hero…it was an older spirit…one from the very end of his run, back when he was so fearfully consumed with bitterness and bigotry, right before his fall down a flight of basement stairs damaged his brain enough to mute his hate…

…Pop had much in common with Kolwaski…he too watched the world he grew up in inexorably surrender to circumstances over which he had little desire to understand…as it was, he did what Kolwaski did- he drank to numb his existence- but like a catch 22, the more he drank to forget, the more he hated what there was left to remember…

…sometimes I'm not sure what he despised more, his world or the fact that he increasingly saw himself playing such an insignificant part in it…Pop's earthly purgatory seemed to be for him to forever rage against the dying of the light, all the while never comprehending that he had spiraled into blindness long ago…

… Pop owned an old Ford…after his accident it sat in front of his house for the better part of a year… one weekend when I was home from Campbell he told me he wanted to see it run one more time…I asked if he wanted to ride in it but he said no…he just want to see the old gal start up and roll again…

…I did finally get it to crank.…managed to drive it around the block and out to the highway- was able to just barely steer the thing into his tiny garage before it gave up the ghost …

…I lied and told him that it drove pretty well…he refused to talk about it and went to bed… I grabbed a six pack, went out into the dark garage and sat in it, smoking and drinkin', listening to the car cool down for the last time…

# Galaxie Christmas

Pop drove a '67 Ford Galaxie 500

an angry lookin', profane beast of an auto
that attacked potholes and railroad tracks alike

broken muffler belching obscenities
as it rumbled through town to a fertilizer factory
where he'd found work after the war
stacking sacks of ammonia nitrate in box cars,

at night the place lit up like Christmas

strings of green and red flashing lights,
huge outdoor industrial lamps
reflecting a fine white powder,

chemical snow that ate car paint like a slow cancer

a year after a headlong plunge down some stairs
killed more brain cells than Korea and the booze ever did

Pop wondered aloud if the engine would turn-
the car hadn't budged since his fall-

with a new Acme battery, eight AC plugs
and a half can of ether sprayed straight into the carb,
she finally fired

the Galaxie groaned as I pulled away from the curb

Pop, watching through the window from his wheelchair,
closed the curtains

we lurched past St. Ann church,
rolling down the block to Bills Bar
for a last look at the old man's second home

I steered her north and headed for 3rd street,
the old gal building up some steam, starting to feel it

pullin' Pop's hard hat tight to my head
I pushed the gas pedal down as far as it would go-

thick black smoke trailing behind us
we charged the last railroad crossing at 70 mph,
leaf springs screaming as we hurled
toward the holiday lights a half mile up the road

…outside again, watching the looming storm, listening to it build…
.I've six small wind chimes hanging from my Bradford Pear tree
branches…all are sounding their tiny alarms…it won't be long…

…I don't know how to paint or draw, at least not on canvas…my
mother was an artist but she denied her talent until her run was about
done- by the time she picked up her brushes she could only see gray,
having become a victim to a lifetime of emotional color blindness…
but she had a gift for painting clouds…watching them so beautiful
and huge against the sky reminds me of her…

 # Artist

Jesus, it was an ugly kitchen-

one 25-watt bulb struggled above her
as she fought

a drunken pugilist
past her prime

mascara streaking
as she struck at the large drawing pad
with frantic strokes

cursing the charcoal
as she ripped the smudged sheets
from the thin spiraled spine
and flung them onto the stained carpet
that matched the yellowed, peeling walls-

"I rolled the Queen Mary" the guy grunted
as he stretched that rug
when we first moved in years ago

while my old man watched, weaving,

and spilt the first of the Seagrams on a visible seam…

…storms without the past couple of days here in central Texas and storms within…been trying to suppress the reaction I had when I came across the photo of a murdered American ambassador being dragged through an African street…

…pushed the pace on a five miler yesterday and ran another hard six miles a little over an hour ago trying to shake it all off- once was a time when I could have kept that up for days and days, but my old bones betray me…cold beer might help, I suppose, along some Coltrane… so far it's all a draw but it won't take much for things to tilt…

…I've never forgotten where I was twenty years ago…

Losing It

hard to forget Mogadishu

drinkin' helps

to lose
the sand and the stench

flies

Four Square Circle

RPG's,

don't need mortars either
especially at night

that goes for tracers, too,

hell

sometimes I just
drink away Sword Base altogether

Shupe's another matter-

Pennsylvanian Master Sergeant

hollow miner's eyes
staring out from beneath his helmet

limping toward me
holding up his hands

like an umpire

fists closed in a full count,

"ten, so far.." he gravels

black words collapsing
like an abandoned shaft,

"maybe more…"

…long, long day…took forever just to get home…crawling along IH 35 in traffic I found myself listening to Lynyrd Skynyrd…"be a simple kind of man"…I wonder if it's too late for that…

…added another VA file folder to my collection of fallen heroes earlier this week… I don't know why I can't bring myself to send the folders to the warehouse…nothing in them except checklists, forms, unrealized dreams…I just can't do it…

…the young veteran student left us this past weekend…was riding his Harley when a pickup truck failed to yield, turning in front of him… this was his first semester at ACC…

…he was enrolled in two motorcycle repair classes, studying to be a bike mechanic- probably wanted to turn his avocation into a vocation- survived a year in Iraq as a wheel vehicle repairer…in a different time, different war he might have been one of my wrenches…the driver of the pickup fled the scene…

…his widow called me this morning…had questions about VA survivor benefits…I gave her the name and phone number of the county Veteran Service Officer…we talked for a little while…she said that it was so unexpected…

…he left behind a young daughter…

…I can still hear the lyrics to the song…"be something you love and understand…"

…nothing's simple…nothing…

Looking for Byzantium

this too is no country for old men-

only the women seem to age,
wizened and stooped,
they sweep at their shadows on the sand

dunes loom large
drifting deep into the darkness

I am back again
patrolling the bypass
that skirts the city

avoiding
the school's scorched, empty lecture halls

shattered Central Bank of Somalia
Semper Fi slashed in red across its coral limestone walls,

the market is vacant

the windmills are still-

I keep my grief at a distance,

traveling east
toward the Old Port

in search of Yeat's dolphin torn
gong tormented sea

…sometimes the words just aren't there- no matter how many different combinations of keys I press, the letters don't reflect on the page what it is I'm trying to say, what I'm trying to get out…it's the damndest thing-

…I can only imagine that it's been a beautiful day- working in an office for eight hours has its price- but I'm home now…lots of familiar sounds in the house- some light jazz floats in the background…dryer's tumbling my PT clothes…every now and then the ice maker dumps a few more cubes, doing its best to keep up…

… I was hoping the few rays of late afternoon sun streaking my kitchen window would warn away my inner shadows-but that old, indefinable mood is hanging around- an "I'm missing something here" feeling… it rests just beyond the reach of my reason…

…my mind is still on the men we lost last week in Afghanistan…I've tried to figure it out- Lord knows I've tried…it made little sense to me all those long years ago in the streets of Mogadishu- it makes less sense to me now…

Fresh Air on NPR

idling at the red
on the corner of Parmer and Lamar

panhandlers with cardboard signs
shuffling up and down the line

my radio program shows me a photo

it's a real beaut-

a profane Pulitzer prize winning snap
of a dead, mutilated American soldier

face up on a dirt road
in Mogadishu

through my Chevy windshield

I watch

the frenzied crowd
drag the bound corpse

past the Citgo station
into the parking lot of the CVS

…well, tomorrow's October 3rd …a long day for me in the best of circumstances- at work by 0700- out the office door at 1630 to teach my organizational behavior class- usually wrapping it all up by 1900 or so…chances are that I'll turn my students loose early…won't tell them why……they couldn't relate, nor could I expect them to…a third of 'em weren't even born in 1993…

…it's too hard to explain it anyway…trust me, I've tried once or twice… to students, to others…to myself…

…took a look at a satellite picture of Mogadishu the other day- found myself doing that same thing I do when I'm sitting out under the arbor, halfway through a six pack- I kept magnifying the image, just like I do in my mind…found myself wondering what I was actually seeing…or why I was looking in the first place…there's a lesson in that, I suppose- I'll file it with all the other unfinished lessons…

…it's a big file…

Harvest Moon

October can be a killing month-

I learned of this
twenty years ago

in Mogadishu-

knew it then

as I know it now,

watching
through the rain-streaked glass of
my kitchen window

a dying tree's leaves
drift to the ground in silence-

were we to see it,

the hidden ringed history of my maple's life
would tell the true story of its struggle,

season by season

once the drought took hold,

it was ever too late-

…there's a former Army paratrooper in my Thursday class, a veteran of Afghanistan and Iraq…he's a good student…as is his practice, last week he arrived early so that we could talk for a while…I mentioned something about the Beirut Bombing anniversary…said that apparently there are many folks still haunted by the tragedy…

…he said that he knew about being haunted- then he confided in me about a ghost of his…

…it seems that the young veteran was point man on a casualty/ remains recovery mission once…a helicopter had crashed…he got the call…

…during the search, he came across what appeared to be a partially rolled up fabric of some sort…he called out to the recovery group coordinator that he'd found something….

…the object was the nearly intact face of a crewman…

…then he said that sometimes in his dreams the face speaks to him… asks if someone could please tell his wife that he's not coming home and that he's sorry that he's left her alone…

…I told my student that I understood his dream…

…that statement is indeed true…

…I told him too, that he's not alone…

…the truth of that observation may be a little more complicated…

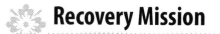

Recovery Mission

late afternoon shadow of the chimney
stretched across the lawn
brought it back

a memory of a mosque at sunset:

tower
silhouette against
a malevolent sky

brown skinned waifs
racing the weary convoy
slinging rocks

old Somali woman in the road
wailing as we creep slowly through the base gate

burned, twisted truck's wreckage in tow

Bangladeshi guard grinning
in the bone yard twilight

...driving home from the gym this afternoon the northern sky was crowded with gray cloud...the weatherman says the cold air is hours away...storms invariably precede the front- seems my restlessness always runs tandem to it...

...I'm thankful, though...here it is, nearly November and I'm able to sit outside sans shirt with a cold beer in hand, watching my old pooch dart around the yard like a pup...she's as oblivious to the looming change in the climate as I wish I might be...my assorted once-broken body parts (foot, fingers, fractured leg) conspire to blame me for their altered condition...fortunately they all respond well to alcohol-based remedies...

...the music of the cicadas is a memory, their departure in concert with the hummingbirds migration...but a chorus of crickets huddled together in the razor grass just behind the arbor are still harmonizing in unison, either celebrating the last warm evening of this extended Texas autumn or singing in spite of tomorrows forecast...

Afternoon Commute

rolling crazy
down the crowded San Antonio-Austin interstate
behind a beat-up crew cab truck
with a rope for a tailgate,

a winch bolted to the bed,

and a small Mexican dude hanging on the hoist chain,
leaning into the erratic lane changes…

saw this once before, in Mogadishu-

Private Munoz in the back of the lead gun truck,
one hand wrapped tight with the sling of
a pedestal-mounted M60,

the other fist gripping a Bic,
trying to light a bent Marlborough,

his arm jerking up and down
like a rodeo rider on a mechanical bucking bull

…I don't know that I would have picked Texas as final settling-down location were it not for my uncle Sam and a creative DOD assignments branch…hard to call it home, even now…but in all fairness I don't think I could call anyplace home except for the Army…I still remember the cadence-

"a home, a home, we've finally found a home"…

…I've met more than my share of old vets lately that could surely use one…had a fellow in yesterday morning- so dirty and disheveled that he left some topsoil on my desk…his DD214 indicated that he'd joined the military right about the time I did back in '74…wanted to tell me he had a different temporary address- a shelter out on Lamar…after he left I couldn't help but think that he might be running out of time… later, staring back at an old man's face in a mirror, I wondered if the same wasn't true of him…

…it's about as winter-looking as it gets here, and almost dark …the backyard Bradford trees stand watch, posted beneath a sliver of moon, just as still and silent as a sentinels…

…shadows of what they used to be…

Standing Watch

I remember
a rare blue moon,

its ascent
bathing the wood
in nocturnal light,

a wolf tree's
splintered shadow of branch
camouflage as I stood watch

listening
to a sound
I could not name,

a child's cry, perhaps,

or
the faint whisper of woodwind chime,

calling me from
this cold, dying timberline

...cold out tonight- winter storm's moving in- not a perfect one but then again, not many storms are...the weatherman says we may have freezing rain and ice- perhaps some thunder-sleet...considering the mood I'm in, I guess it's perfect enough...

...my sister sent me a gift last week- she could not imagine how rare it is...all the letters my father wrote to my mother during the Korean War...some of them are so beautifully poignant as to break one's heart...they reveal much...

...one evident truth, expressed in every single letter was that my father was deeply in love with my mother...

...I don't know if that truth survived his return from combat...

...but there is another one, still residing between the lines and not nearly so recognizable- that the war was damaging my father beyond measure-

...that truth surely thrived...

...on Christmas day in 1993 I landed at Campbell Army Airfield, right off a battlefield that no one gave a damn about...I was angry, hurt, frustrated, disappointed, confused, bitter...lost...

...on Christmas day in 1950, on a ship steaming south from the just-destroyed port of Hungnam my father scribbled out a letter to his young bride- said that we'd been badly beaten by the Chinese and that he was sorry...wrote that he knew he shouldn't talk about things like that but he didn't know who else to tell and he had to tell someone...

...I'm still thinking about that letter...

Unfriendly Exfil

from beneath the cover of a Cobra

as 5-ton cargos
hauled us
down the empty bypass to the airport

I took one look back at Mogadishu-

I don't know why
but

I thought about

the man
who
could peer
down

at a town
from a plane

and later draw the whole thing from memory

all the ugly alleys

collapsed walls

shattered windows...

an old Stepphenwolf song still plays in my head-

get your motor running,
head out on the highway

fire all your guns at once

…this world can be a lonely place sometimes…make no mistake though- everyone's movin' through it one way or the other-they just don't know it, or perhaps they do but they'd rather not believe it…

…some folks have the opinion that they're firmly in control of their own destiny- they can slow things down or speed things up as they see fit…ah, but that's not really how it is…truth be told, we're all well on our way toward another destination- we just don't get to handle the throttle or the brake…everyone gets to ride, all right- there's just no sense asking the conductor how long till the next stop…

…I remember one early summer evening when I was a kid, sittin' on the side porch with the old man, sippin' a beer like a grownup, savoring every bit of it and wishing I could get up enough nerve to ask him for a smoke…a storm was coming in and I could see the lightning off in the distance…we listened to a freight train blow it's whistle as it approached the Locust street crossing…seemed like that note just hung in the air forever…Pop said that the humidity helped carry the sound…hours later I imagined that I could still hear it…

…some evening whether you're sittin' in your backyard looking up at the stars or whether you're on your apartment balcony lookin' down at the street below- listen hard for a train whistle- imagine that it's all of our fallen heroes telling the rest of us that they're on their way… letting us know that they're not alone…

Behind Me

need
to leave behind
the grimy flak jacket

such a worthless garment

stiff with sand and grit
ever rubbing raw the back of my neck,

the smoldering mix
of diesel fuel and burn pit refuse

acrid smoke hanging like a premonition
over the base

the endless dirge of discharging ordnance-

remember instead
a late fall afternoon

a basketball's
warm ringing bounce

echoing clang of an errant shot
off a loose rim

dry wake of burnished leaves
as I raced shadows down
empty avenue sidewalks

silently counting strides
from streetlight to streetlight

chasing the plumed vapor
of my labored breathing

sprinting for home across
Spencer ball field

bright with harvest moon

Printed in the United States
By Bookmasters